D0820553

3 9101 00019 0422

Norwood Public Library
1110 Lucerne Street
Norwood, CO 81423

Published by Creative Education
P.O. Box 227, Mankato, Minnesota 56002
Creative Education is an imprint of
The Creative Company
www.thecreativecompany.us

Design and production by The Design Lab
Art direction by Rita Marshall
Printed in the United States of America

Photographs by Corbis (Norbert Wu/Science
Faction), Getty Images (John Giustina, Beverly
Joubert, Stan Osolinski, Panoramic Images, Valerie
Shaff, Anup Shah, Paul Souders, Art Wolfe,
iStockphoto (David T. Gomez, Eric Isselée)

Copyright © 2010 Creative Education
International copyright reserved in all countries.
No part of this book may be reproduced in any
form without written permission from the publisher.

Library of Congress Cataloging-in-Publication Data
Bodden, Valerie.
Lions / by Valerie Bodden.
p. cm. — (Amazing animals)
Includes bibliographical references and index.
Summary: A basic exploration of the appearance,
behavior, and habitat of lions, the majestic big cats
of Africa and India. Also included is a story from
folklore explaining why lions roar.
ISBN 978-1-58341-807-9
1. Lions—Juvenile literature. I. Title. II. Series.
QL737.C23B6428 2010
599.757—dc22   2009002709

First Edition
9 8 7 6 5 4 3 2 1

AMAZING ANIMALS

LIONS

BY VALERIE BODDEN

CREATIVE EDUCATION

Lions are big cats. They are the second-largest cats in the world. Only tigers grow bigger than lions.

Lions live in hot areas that have a lot of grass

Lions have a strong body covered with fur. The fur can be yellow or brown. Lions have a long tail, big teeth, and sharp claws. Male lions have a mane. A mane is an area of bushy hair around the lion's head and neck.

A mane makes a male lion look even bigger

Male lions are about eight feet (2.4 m) long. They weigh more than two grown-up men put together! Female lions are a little smaller.

Male lions are stronger, but females are faster

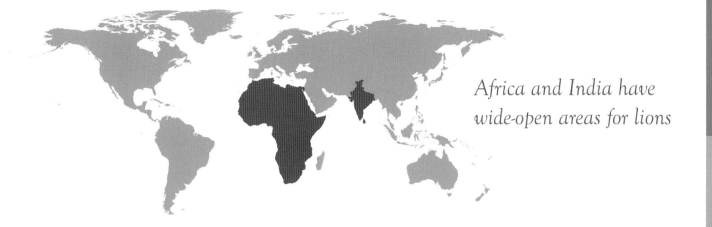

Africa and India have wide-open areas for lions

Many lions live on **savannas**. Others live in dry forests. Most lions live on the **continent** of Africa. A few lions live in India. They are called Asiatic (*ay-zhe-AT-ick*) lions.

savannas flat, hot lands covered with grass and a few trees

continent one of Earth's seven big pieces of land

Lions eat other animals. Some of their favorite animals to eat are zebras, wildebeest, and antelopes. Sometimes lions even eat elephants! A few lions have eaten people.

A lion may eat 75 pounds (34 kg) of meat at once

Female lions keep careful watch over their cubs

A mother lion has two to six cubs at a time. At first, the cubs stay in a den with their mother. When the cubs are about five weeks old, they leave the den. They begin to learn how to hunt. Lions in the wild can live about 15 years.

cubs baby lions

den a home that is hidden, like a cave

Lions live in family groups called prides. Most prides have about 15 lions. The lions of a pride spend a lot of time sleeping. Lions sleep and rest about 20 hours a day! Cubs spend a lot of time playing.

Lions like to rest during the hottest times of day

Lions move around the most at night. Sometimes they roar as they move around. Lions often hunt at night. Female lions do most of the hunting. They usually work together as a team.

Lions look for sick or old animals to catch and eat

Today, people around the world go to zoos to see lions. Some people watch lions perform in the circus. And some people even go to Africa to see lions in the wild. It is exciting to get close to these big cats!

Zoo lions and wild lions like to spend time playing

A Lion Story

Why do lions roar? People in Africa used to tell a story about this. They said that the lion used to sneak up on animals and eat them. One day, a **hare** put honey from a beehive on the lion while he slept. When the bees saw the honey, they stung the lion. The pain made the lion roar. From then on, the lion roared, and the animals always heard him coming!

hare an animal that looks like a rabbit but is bigger

Read More

Petty, Kate. *Lions*. Mankato, Minn.: Stargazer Books, 2005.

Rennert, Violette. *Little Lions*. Milwaukee: Gareth Stevens Publishing, 2006.

Web Sites

Enchanted Learning: Lions
http://www.enchantedlearning.com/subjects/mammals/lion/coloring.shtml
This site has lion facts and a picture to color.

National Geographic Kids Creature Feature: Lions
http://kids.nationalgeographic.com/Animals/CreatureFeature/Lion
This site has pictures and videos of lions.

Index

LIONS